Psyche

"Pavita Singh's latest volume of poetry, *Psyche*, is a kaleidoscope of imagery that encompasses mental health, travel, self-care, female empowerment, and personal growth. It is a celebration of self, life, and looking at the world through eyes filled with hope and wonder. In brilliant technicolor, Pavita Singh spreads her wings in this collection of verses and allows us a glimpse into the heart and mind of a girl who wanders."

—Crystal Jackson,
poet, author of Heart of Madison series

"In a follow-up as honest and gentle as *To All the Magic in Me*, Pavita Singh invites the readers to continue their exploration of her mind and heart. Throughout the project, Singh masterfully carries you through a mindful walk of her own, peppered with little stops along the way that point to some of the struggles and desires we can all relate to as women, as adults, and ultimately, as human beings."

—N. Williams,
multimedia artist, author of *Cotton*

"Pavita Singh is full of surprises, and this new collection of poetry, *Psyche*, is no exception. As soon as we get to 'Cannot Breathe,' it becomes apparent that she has departed for distant shores in both her thoughts and her settings, and we are the ones who get all the feelings and all the scenery."

—Billy Manas,
author of *Kickass Recovery: From Your First Year Clean to the Life of Your Dreams*

"Immediately heartfelt, heartbreaking, honest, and pure, *Psyche* pulls the complex emotions of *To All the Magic in Me* and pushes them outward into the world. Pavita Singh passionately paints the self as a mosaic, a vastness of stained glass exposed—our emotions, thoughts, and experiences shifting in and out of the light, and just as beautiful in darkness. A must-read to accept, to smile, to reflect, to escape, and to heal."

—Susan Morrison,
Georgia Public Library Services

"Pavita Singh's words wind up the trees and down through the soul, evoking worlds and words that give flight to the beauty in the unspoken."

—Christine Horansky,
author of *Girl Power in the Age of Millennials: Essays on Youth, Women, and Global Social Change*

Psyche

Dear Maddie ~
Spread your wings & fly!
Love. ~ Paula

Psyche

A POETIC JOURNEY THROUGH THE BODY, MIND, SOUL, AND PLANET

PAVITA SINGH, MPH

Illustrations by Mary K. Biswas

PSYCHE
Copyright © 2023 Pavita Singh
All rights reserved.

Published by Publish Your Gift®
An imprint of Purposely Created Publishing Group, LLC

Printed in the United States of America
ISBN: 978-1-64484-620-9 (print)
ISBN: 978-1-64484-621-6 (ebook)

To the Universe.

To my biological family and my soul family.

To my spiritual journey and all my travel companions I've met along the way—you know who you are!

To all the magic in me.

Thank you.

Table of Contents

Preface xiii

Introduction 1

My Wings 5

Beautiful: Ode to a Pen 7

My Pen Is a Magic Wand 8

Cannot Breathe 10

One Percent 12

Privilege 14

A Cup of Coffee 16

Censorship 17

Palette 18

Ocean of Emotions 24

Henna Artist 25

Blood 26

Princess 27

Lend a Hand 29

Stairways to My Soul 30

Shut Up, New York 33

The Presents of Presence 36

Vicious Cycle 38

More Than the Squares 39

Low Battery 41

What Are You Doing There? 42

Empowered Woman... 43

My Best Friend and My Worst Enemy.................. 45

Turn off the Lights... 47

City Lights 48

Power of the Page 49

Don't Be a Jerk 51

Date Night 52

My Love Is Mine 54

Butterfly Garden 56

Lovemaking of the Soul....................................... 57

Overdue Thank You Notes 58

A Thousand Lifetimes.. 61

To My Weak Nails 62

Not Alone 64

Snapshot... 65

Brave... 66

Crayon Box... 69

Is It Wrong? 73

Why I Write... 75

I'm Not a Tourist.. 76

Water 79

Storybook Collection 81

To Love a Girl Who Wanders 82

Always There.. 85

Artist 87

What Do You Do? 88

Listen to the Kids.. 89

Ramona Street... 91

Loving Kindness 93

Keep to Myself 95

Dance Class 96

A Day in the Life of an Editor................... 98

Breath.. 100

Pure Love.. 101

Girls' Night Out 102

A Love Letter to the Upper East Side................... 104

Sunset.. 107

11:11 109

Butterfly Pose 110

References.. 113

About the Author 115

Preface

I was exhausted. Despite getting my usual eight hours of sleep, I couldn't stay awake. My eyes were drooping. I felt like I was going to fall as I was walking.

I am no stranger to fatigue. I have struggled with the condition for years, so much so that I was unable to get through most days without a nap in my early twenties. I would take naps in the relaxation room at my office, and while my boss didn't necessarily mind, she was concerned. She recommended that I talk to an ayurvedic practitioner we both knew who would help me get my energy levels way up. Since then, I have still loved my naps, but I do not depend on them the way I used to.

That weekend, however, was different. It was an early afternoon in September 2022, and I didn't know how I was going to get through the day. I was on vacation in Providence and Newport, Rhode Island, enjoying the change of season and getting a reprieve from the chaos of New York City life. Out of desperation, I had a cup of cappuccino. I never have coffee. And guess what. It didn't even help.

What was going on? Were there any changes in my diet or lifestyle? Not that I could think of. Well, other than the possibility of applying to doctoral programs.

I messaged my ayurvedic practitioner with my symptoms. She replied, "Let's rule out three things: COVID, iron or vitamin deficiency, and pregnancy."

"Ha!" I thought to myself. I hadn't gotten any action in over two years. I could not conceivably be pregnant (pun entirely intended). As for the other possibilities, I would have to figure that out later.

As I walked through the gardens of the Vanderbilt Mansion in Newport, Rhode Island, I felt restless. My muscles were achy. Bursts of creativity came gushing at me. It seemed that I was having metaphorical contractions.

As it turns out, I *was* pregnant.

With a book.

I rushed to the museum gift shop, purchased a journal, started writing, and immediately felt relief.

May you enjoy the result.

Introduction

Mariposa. Papillon. Farfalla. Schmetterling. Titalee.

Written above is the same word in multiple languages—languages that at various points have been an important part of my life and have brought out different aspects of my personality. The warmth, sexiness, and late-night parties of Spanish. The elegance and creativity of French. The romance, savoriness, flowiness, and music of Italian. The science, innovation, routine, and organization of German. The familial community, liveliness, spice, and social activism of Punjabi.

That word is butterfly.

I have always thought of myself as a butterfly—a beautiful, free-spirited creature fluttering and frolicking about, never quite sure exactly where I'm going but trusting the universe to guide my wings and knowing I'll spread my magic wherever I end up.

One such instance of fluttering and frolicking serendipitously landed me in Athens, Georgia in February 2018. On this excursion, I recognized one of my soul companions. Although it was our first meeting as humans in this lifetime, we both almost immediately realized the significance of our connection. In this fourteen-hour meeting, we spent time getting to know each other and, being the nerds we both are, delved into conversations about languages, literature, geography, history, botany, politics, philosophy, sociology, and psychology. In addition to being soul companions, we also deemed ourselves "psyche mates"—a term that we came up with because the word "psyche" encompasses not only the spirit, but also the mind.

When I returned home to California, where I was living at the time, I sent this soul companion/psyche mate a painting I made of a butterfly as an appreciation for the short but meaningful time we spent together on my trip. The painting was accompanied by a note that explained that the butterfly represented me; even though I had to quickly fly away (in this case, both literally and figuratively), I would eventually fly back if and when the time was right. In the meantime, thanks to smartphones and text messaging, we stayed in contact.

Inevitably, we had many conversations all about butterflies—the actual creature and the translation of the word in the various languages listed above. It has always fascinated me that despite all being Indo-European languages, the word "butterfly" in these languages do not seem to bear any resemblance to one another (except, perhaps, for *farfalla* and *papillon*) and all evoke for me such different imagery. Even so, I love and feel connected to each of the above translations of "butterfly," no matter how different. For fun, we decided one day to look up the word for "butterfly" in ancient Greek, a language to which my soul companion/psyche mate has long felt connected.

And guess what.

The word is psyche.[1]

Many cultures and civilizations throughout human history have viewed the butterfly as a symbol of the soul, thus the word psyche—the ancient Greek word for soul.[2, 3] Psyche also means "breath" or "to breathe," hence "to live," in ancient Greek.[4] In Greek mythology, Psyche was also the name of Eros's (the god of love) human lover.[5] Therefore, the butterfly has also become a symbol for life and love. Other concepts represented by the butterfly include beauty, transience, transformation, growth, inner trust and wisdom, positivity, overcoming obstacles, embracing one's uniqueness, and the balance between being grounded and free-floating.[6]

Due to my research on butterflies combined with my personal life experiences, the motif of the butterfly has taken on additional meanings for me to the ones above. Some of these meanings include appreciation of life's simple pleasures; women's empowerment; wanderlust; healing; creativity; imagination;

limitless possibility; and the interconnection among the body, mind, and spirit. All of these ideas, along with the literal image of the butterfly, are woven into the words of *Psyche: A Poetic Journey Through the Body, Mind, Soul, and Planet.*

The poems in this collection span various periods of my life from 2005 to 2023. Just as in my debut poetry collection, *To All the Magic in Me: A Collection of Love Letters to All of Life's Emotions*, the poems in *Psyche* illustrate the complexity, contradiction, evolution, messiness, and magic that it means to be alive.

Let's fly in!

My Wings

You were my cocoon.
My first home in this lifetime.
The site of my transformation
From the spiritual realm
To the physical world.
The provider of my wings.

My first hug, my first kiss.
My first tear.
My first meal.
My first pain and my first heal.
My first smile, my first laugh.
My first toy, my first school.
My first teacher, counselor, and nurse.
My first heartbreak, my first curse.
My first sight and my first fight.

My first love and my first friend
Until the very end.
Throughout all lifetimes, this love will transcend.

Our relationship is the most challenging,
Yet also the strongest.
I feel your pain as it is mine—
The result of two bodies
Becoming one
Becoming two again.

Your love is the source of my life.
The source of my love—
All the love I have
For myself, for others, for the world.
The source of my strength.
The source of my wings
To make this world my own.

Beautiful: Ode to a Pen[7]

This poem was originally published on elephant journal.

A blank sheet of paper,
White as snow
Just waiting to be filled
With feelings of love,
Pain, and excitement.
My pen glides across the paper,
Leaving behind permanent marks
With some perfections,
Some mistakes,
Just as an ice skater
Mellifluously skates across the ice
Making shapes that will
Forever freeze
With some falls here and there.
This, to me, is
Beautiful.

My Pen Is a Magic Wand

I am a sorceress
With magical powers.
My pen is a magic wand,
And it can manifest anything.

With my words,
I cast spells,
Enchanting
The minds and hearts
Of readers near and far.
I can influence opinions.
Create new worlds.
Give birth to characters.

Make or break reputations.
Nurture relationships.
Educate.
Entertain.
Empower.
Heal.
All with some smudges
Of ink on paper.

I always try to use
My powers for good,
But if you ever hurt me
Or anyone I love,
My words will come for you.

I am a sorceress
With magical powers.
My pen is a magic wand,
And it can manifest anything.

Cannot Breathe

This poem is based on the real-life experiences of girls and young women in India.

When she was young,
This was not how she imagined this day.
The morning of her wedding,
She is mourning.
Her mother ties her sari
So tightly that her tummy looks round,
So tightly that her breasts look plump,
So tightly that she cannot breathe.
Her aunt presses on her teeth,
So hard that they will never protrude.
She looks into the mirror
And cannot recognize herself,
For her tears are the only things real.
She thinks to herself,
"I want to be in love."
She does not love him.
He knows his brother rapes her,
He knows his father beats her,
He knows his mother burns her,
Yet she cannot say no,

For her parents will not want her,
Her family will not want her,
Nobody in this village will want her.
She will never be independent,
She will never learn to read,
She will never be able to get out of being her in-laws' slave.
This is what the rest of her life looks like.
She will never be able to breathe again.

One Percent

Even if someone leaves my life
Or I leave from theirs
Because a relationship no longer serves
Doesn't mean that they're not still part of my
psyche.
That's the thing about having a photographic
memory.
It's my greatest blessing and greatest curse.
It is physically impossible for me to forget.
Being blocked from my phone
Doesn't translate to being blocked from my mind.
While ninety-nine percent of me feels relief
That I'm not interacting with them regularly,
If at all,
There's still that one percent of space
That's occupied by anger.
Nostalgia.
Compassion.
Lessons.
Questions.
The one percent that compels me to reach out
On birthdays

Or death anniversaries,
At least for the first year.
The one percent that reminds me
That I'm not a robot
Or a computer
That can simply delete a file
And have it erased from memory
But a human.
As messy and irritating as that space is,
That one percent
Is where I want to be.

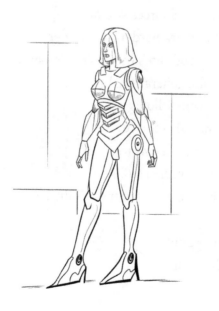

Privilege

Is privilege truly privilege?
Or is it instead pressure?
Pressure to reflect on the state of the world
And your place in it.
The contributions you intend to make.
Pressure to navigate the balance between
Maintaining the status quo for yourself
And breaking it for others
So they, too, may enjoy access
To the same resources you do.
Pressure to work harder and harder
To keep up with life's increasing demands
And provide generational wealth
For those who follow
So they may also thrive
In a world that seems to get
Ever more complicated.
With privilege comes responsibility.
Stress.
Sometimes guilt.
The realization

That in the blink of an eye,
It can all vanish.
So is privilege truly privilege?
Or is it instead pressure?

A Cup of Coffee

Over the decades, lots has changed in our lives,
But are we truly thriving, or just aiming to survive?
DMs, short texts, typing on computers,
What ever happened to pen and paper?
Sitting all day in front of screens for business calls,
What ever happened to walking or going out and
playing ball?
All the work and all the stress,
What ever happened to time to rest?
People just work from day's start to day's end,
Why not take some time off and enjoy coffee with a
friend?

Censorship

Sometimes being successful
Requires censorship.
Hiding certain parts of yourself.
What you really think.
How you really feel.
What you really enjoy.
I say fuck censorship.
How can anything change
Unless we're honest about what's wrong?
How can we form relationships
Without showing people who we are?
Why should I have to censor myself
Just to make others comfortable?
If what I have to say or do
Is too much for them to bear,
Then maybe they don't belong in my tribe
Nor am I the right fit for theirs.

Palette

My soul is a palette.
A canvas.
A collection of clashing, contrasting colors.
My soul is a mosaic
With messy, mismatching pieces
Of varying shapes, sizes, and styles
Mashed together,
Appearing unaesthetic on the surface,
But all necessary.
All part of me.
All perfectly imperfect,
And therefore all beautiful.

I am the fiery passion of red.
The livid ire that recognizes injustices and issues
And is driven to inspire change.
I am the expletives and explosion,
The blood from my inner fight,
The glowing flame burning bright
That keeps me moving,
Propels me forward,
No matter the circumstances.

I am the ebb and flow of the ocean waves.
The glistening, crystal-clear blue.
The cool breeze that dances across the skin
And gives the mind permission to close its eyes,
Take a deep breath,
Inhale the brisk freshness of the air,
Exhale peace into the world,
And just relax.

I am the dark storm clouds
Crying a rainfall of tears.
The grey smoke expelling toxic waste
Of the trauma and hurt
I've harbored inside for too long,
Leaving behind dusty ashes and powdery soot,

Making me sick to my stomach,
Forcing me to purge
What no longer serves.

I am the lush green vegetation
Whose thirst has been quenched by rain.
I am able to exude vibrancy,
As I know what it's like to feel pain.
I am the healthy, natural food
That comes straight from the womb of Mother
Earth,
Providing nourishment, healing, growth, and
abundance
To myself and all living beings.

I am the thick, sticky mud.
Viscous clumps of opaque brown
That stall movement.
I am stuckness.
Writer's block.
Blurred vision.
Depression.
Sheer exhaustion.
Unsure where I'm going next,
Yet somehow managing

To build up my strength and endurance
And slowly trudge my way through.

I am a burst of sunlight
Whose bright yellow rays shimmer through the sky
And bring warmth.
Comfort.
Energy.
Fun.
Rejuvenation.
The urge to let loose and dance.
Pure bliss and excitement
Simply about being alive.

I am the timeless, classic elegance of black
With a unique ability
To make bold statements
Without uttering a word
And to inspire awe
And leave a permanent mark on the world
Solely by virtue of my existence.

I am innocence and virginity.
A crisp, fresh sheet of white paper.
A blank slate.

A beginner's mind
Experiencing the wonders of life
As if for the first time.
I absorb all my surroundings
And constantly create myself.

And I am the pretty, perky positivity of pink.
I am friendship, lust, and romance.
I am universal, unconditional love.
I am glitter and glam.
I am connection.
Confidence.
Nurturing, divine femininity.
Gentle flower petals.
A sweet reminder
That no matter how hard life gets,
Everything will be just fine.

I hold in me everything good in the world,
But also everything bad.
My colors don't always mesh
Or work well together,
But they all need one another.
Even though I don't always like every part of me,
I will never mask anything

Or try to smooth the rough edges of my mosaic,
My inner garden and my rainbow,
For I love my palette
Of clashing, contradictory, contrasting colors.
My beautifully messy,
Authentic
Self.

Ocean of Emotions

The heart is an ocean of emotions,
A pool of passions,
A shower of secrets,
A lagoon of love.
This ocean of emotions
Is more powerful than the Pacific,
Though something can sink into it
And still be preserved
For many years—even eternity.
Whatever you do,
You must keep this ocean safe,
For without it, you have nothing.

Henna Artist

Few activities
Make me feel present
Or at peace.
But when applying paste
To the hands and feet,
Painting intricate patterns
Of paisley, hearts, flowers,
Peacock feathers, fractals,
Butterflies,
Obsessing over minute details,
Sharing stories on the skin,
No other thoughts
Occupy my mind.
Nothing else matters.
I feel at ease.
In the flow.
Focused.
Free.
And know that all is fine.

Blood

Two thirds of girls around the world
Have no idea what's happening to them
The first time they see blood
Between their legs.
Why is it that they've never been taught
Or that they're given false information
That makes them terrified
To bleed each month?
Like that they can't eat what they want,
Pray when they want,
Or play whatever and with whomever they want?
What's worse, they might miss days of school,
Turning their menstrual cycle
Into a vicious cycle
Of poverty and abuse.
Girls, your bleeding doesn't make you weaker.
In fact, it makes you stronger.
There is power in your blood,
As it's the source of all life.
Tap into and embrace that power.

Princess

Poor little princess
Trapped in her dark, black tower.
Suffering.
Oppressed.
Cannot express.
Encompassed completely,
The poor princess has no power,
Nor anyone to answer
Her pleas for escape.
To go out in the streets and see the world.
To see letters and understand what they mean.

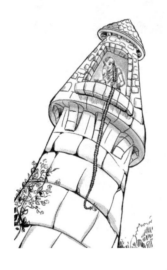

To think for herself and not just accept what she's
told.
To know she can do more than cook and clean.
No matter how much she yells,
She's but a quiet mouse
A voice that is spoken over
By the fathers and brothers of the house.
Poor little princess
Wishing her surrounding tower could vanish,
Letting down her long, thick carpet of hair,
Showing the world she's free.

Lend a Hand

In this world, some of us have it so well,
But there are others who don't, you can definitely
tell.
While some may be used to money and caviar,
Others can't go to school or go very far.
Good fortune shouldn't be taken for granted,
And each time we help someone, the world is
mended.
So why not give the homeless people some food
Or spend time with someone struggling and
brighten their mood?
When people help others, the world is a better
place,
But we can't wait to get started, we must pick up the
pace.
It's extremely important, the truth must be told,
For when you lend a hand, you cleanse your own
soul.

Stairways to My Soul

My soles
The stairways to my soul
Taking in information about the world
As I walk across the Earth
Exploring all its corners,
Its mountains, hills, and valleys,
Its smooth sidewalks and rough terrains,
Its lush green grass and stone-covered alleys.

My soles
The stairways to my soul
With their unique shape
The curves of my arches
The lines and creases telling a story
Of journeys, of marches.
The blisters and calluses from dance
Expressing myself through movement across the
floor.
The softness from my daily self-care,
Coming back to myself.

My soles
The stairways to my soul
Keeping me strong and grounded with mountain
pose and warrior one
Keeping me balanced and flexible
Allowing me to reach new limits
And always come home.

My satisfied soles
The stairways to my soul
Knuckles dug deep into my heels
Making firm arcs in my arches
Penetrating profoundly into my tissues
My muscles
My bones
My soul
Every single cell of my body.
Pulling on my toes
Taking away the toxins of the day
Reminding me everything will be okay
Relaxing me, putting me at ease
Till I fall into a restful slumber.

My prescient soles
The stairways to my soul
Traveling millions of miles
Through cities, fields, beaches, and gardens
Up and down steps
Leading me
Exactly where I am meant to be.

Shut Up, New York[2]

This poem was written in 2020 at the peak of the COVID-19 pandemic. It was originally published on Medium.

Dear New York,
I fell in love with your energy,
Your vibrancy,
Your joie de vivre.
You are so beautiful with your glimmering lights,
The shape of your landscape,
Your ability to adapt to every mood.
Day or night, you always had something to offer.
You would never cease to please.

New York,
The infatuation has worn off.
I love you, and I always will,
But I am irritated and enraged.
You are not the city with which I fell in love.
You are needlessly loud.
Even from twenty-four floors above,
Supposedly my safe space,
My sanctuary,
I hear your yells and cries,

Your shrieking screams,
Your blaring sirens and horns,
Your roaring engines
Multiple times a day
Every day.
Why?

New York,
You must be hurting and crying for help.
Is noise the answer?
If you just took a moment to pause and breathe,
Oh, how much noise could be avoided!

New York,
I am tired.
You have aged me thirty years in thirty weeks.
New York, you have ruined me for life.
Because you have me trapped.
You won't let me go.
As mad as I am at you right now,
I can't go anywhere else.
Can I?
I will never find a place quite like you.
You are like a drug,

And I'm addicted to you.
I can't get your high anywhere else.

New York,
You're supposed to be home.
But this is not home,
This is exhaustion.
This is not peace,
This is disruption.
Just as you're hurting,
You're hurting me too.
Shut up, New York.
Heal and please just shut up.

The Presents of Presence

"What do you want for your birthday?" they ask.
I don't need presents.
I just want presence.
Let's go out for food
To set the mood
Share stories over champagne
Then come home and play games.
All night, we'll joke and laugh,
Look at old photos, reminisce about the past,
Maybe sing and dance
If we get a chance.

Things come and go,
That's something I know,
But just being together
Will leave an impact forever.
That's how we'll celebrate.
Doesn't it sound great?
So come over, let's chill,
Talk about the serious and the nonsense.
I don't need presents.
I just want presence.

Vicious Cycle

If someone has hurt you,
Just remember
That more than likely,
It's not because of you,
But because of them.
Because sometime in the past,
They have been hurt by someone else.
Hurt people hurt people.
If you are hurting,
You owe it to yourself
And to all those who follow
To heal.
Take care of yourself.
Love yourself
So that you may in turn love others
And at once break the vicious cycle
Of perpetual turmoil and destruction.
Don't hurt.
Heal.

More Than the Squares[9]

This poem was originally published on Medium.

You look at the squares,
And you see me.
The story of my life.
As if it could neatly fit inside those tiny boxes.

You see multiple squares coming together,
Forming a quilt.
A beautiful, colorful tapestry.
A more complex picture.
But still incomplete.

Do you think you can see the squares and know
me?
You can try, but you can't.
You never will.
I am more than the squares.
I am more than the sum of the squares.

No matter how much I weave,
The quilt will never be finished.
Will never cover the full, beautiful, complex, messy,
evolving, magical mosaic that is me.
Do you ever wonder what happens outside the
squares?
Let's talk.

Low Battery

When I see my phone battery
Approach 10 percent,
I panic,
As if the oxygen is being sucked out of me,
At the prospect
Of being disconnected,
Stuck,
Lost,
Unreachable,
Inconvenienced,
Even if temporarily,
And rush to find an outlet
To recharge
And reconnect.
Isn't it interesting
That I don't always feel
That same urgency
Towards my own body?

What Are You Doing There?

When I travel,
People like to ask,
"What are you doing there?"
"What's there?"
"What brings you there?"
"What's the purpose of your visit?"
Or the like.
Sometimes I have an answer
Before I arrive,
But more often,
I do not.
I just wander
And land wherever
The universe draws me in,
Allowing myself to simply be
And letting the answers come to me.

Empowered Woman[10]

This poem was originally published on Medium.

I am an empowered woman.
I may not be who you want me to be,
But I am no less empowered than you.

I like showing off my body.
My winding roads, mountains, and valleys,
My speed bumps, potholes, and grassy patches.
I like putting on a tank top,
Exposing my skin,
Turning up the music,
And seducing my audience with my movement.
I may not be modest or reserved,
But I am no less empowered than you.

I like being spoiled and pampered
Having every whim tended to.
I like giving myself to someone I trust
And being dominated behind closed doors.
Sometimes I get excited by derogatory song lyrics,
Seemingly demeaning as they might be.

I am not ashamed of my tastes and preferences,
And I am no less empowered than you.

I embrace my sexuality.
My sensuality.
My creative expression.
My free spirit.
I know my quirks and imperfections,
Yet I still choose not to hide any part of me.
I am no less empowered than you.

It is not my job to make you comfortable
Or fit into your tiny box
Your idea of what an empowered woman
should be.
What I like and what I do
Are not a reflection on you.
I do not live my life for you.
I live for nobody but me.

I am an empowered woman.
I may not be who you want me to be,
But I am no less empowered than you.

My Best Friend and
My Worst Enemy"

This poem was originally published on Medium.

My every morning starts with you,
And my every night ends with you.
Heck, my nights don't even end with you.
I always sleep next to you
And occasionally play with you in the middle of the
night.
I could stare at you for hours on end,
And run my fingers all over you,
And make you do anything for me.

I need you in my life.
Without you, it's hard to survive.
At times, I am literally lost without you.
Wherever I go, you're always by my side.
The way you light up has such power over me.

I love you.

And I also hate you.

You demand so much attention.
Want so much from me at once.
You disturb my peace with your noises.

Yet you make it so difficult to ignore you.
Leaving you unattended fills me with anxiety
Because you need me as much as I need you,
Don't you?

No.

You do not.

Yes, I am addicted to you.
But I'm learning to put myself before you,
Phone.
I'm learning it's okay to stay away.

Turn off the Lights

Turning on the lights at night
Dependent on the light for sight
Thinking that the lights are right.

We turn to electricity,
Artificial colors,
To give us the sight we seek.
They might.

But when we turn on our
human-made lights,
We block out the stars.
The universe's light.
The soul's answers.

Human-made light may give temporary solace,
But the stars reveal our true path.

So one night,
You might just turn off the lights
And look to the stars
For the universe's guidance,
The path that is right.

City Lights[12]

This poem was originally published on Medium.

Looking out the window,
Or walking down the street,
Enamored by bright, sparkling lights
Bringing the city to life.
Tiny particles of glimmering color,
Each telling their own stories.
Stories of talks around the table
And home-cooked meals.
Of cozying up on the couch with popcorn and a movie.
Of late nights curled up with a book
Or scrambling to meet a tight deadline.
Of candles burning during passionate sex.
Of journeys across bridges.
City lights
Making micro rainbows in the water and the sky,
Keeping people safe,
All coming together,
And creating magic.

Power of the Page[13]

This poem was originally published on Medium.

Opening a book
Is a sacred act.
The pages flutter
Like butterfly wings,
Flying near and far,
Connecting author and audience,
Pen and page,
Across time and space.

Opening a book
Opens minds
Opens hearts
Forming friendships from afar
Finding oneself in the words.

Opening a book
Makes a tree's soul smile
Knowing it has been reincarnated
Into eternal life.

That is the power of the page.

Don't Be a Jerk

When did basic human decency
Become such a rare commodity?
Why is it so hard
To not be a jerk?
Hard as it may be to believe,
No one is more important
Than anyone else.
No one owes you anything.
No one is above respect and kindness.

Date Night

I want to roll around with you
Enmesh myself with you
Curl up with you
And a good book.
Lights out.
Candles lit.
Wine glasses clinking.
Starting with some Shakespearean sonnets.
Parsing the pentameter.
The psyche's erotica.
Followed by frolicking into philosophy.
Windy excursions into human history.

I want to lie awake.
Talk. Debate.
Caffeinated with conversation.
Parlance about prose. Politics. Poets. People.
Passion. Progress.
I want to uncover your ideas as I uncover you.
Fucking with our brains before our bodies.

I want to hold you by the shoulders,
My bare legs wrapping around your naked torso,
All your weight on top of me.
You run your hands through my hair,
Tug on it gently as you lick my lips,
The tips of our tongues touching.

I want you to own me as you penetrate me
With ravaging,
Spicy,
Sweaty,
Flaming,
Ardent,
Mind-blowing,
Exciting
SEX.

Then back to lexicon.

My Love Is Mine[14]

This poem was originally published on Medium.

You think I don't care.
You say it's not love.
But if that were true,
Then why do I feel like a part of me is missing?
Why is your absence weighing on me?
Why am I doing the things we did together
Alone
Wondering what you're doing?
How you're doing?
Why am I carrying guilt for the things I did and said
Knowing that they've hurt you?
Why am I crying
Knowing the same tears are flowing from you?

You say it's not love,
You believe it's just words,
But I know how I feel.
Love is my truth.
Your love is yours.
My love is mine.

Drastically different in appearance,
But no less real.

Right now, we are apart,
Not because I don't love you,
But instead because I love me too.

Your love is yours.
My love is mine.
Mine may not be the same,
But it's no less true.

Butterfly Garden

My mind is a butterfly garden
With thoughts flying aimlessly.
No matter how much I try to tame them,
Whether through meditation or yoga or
breathwork,
They wander as they wish,
Sometimes spiraling out of control,
Ending up in places they probably shouldn't,
Finding predators and pesticides.
But the wise butterflies understand
That everything is transient,
And they continue to flutter
Until they find their flowers
Or eventually fade away.

Lovemaking of the Soul

The movement of the pen
Is lovemaking at its purest—
The lovemaking of the soul.
The pen thrusts itself,
Stripping the psyche of all its layers
To its rawest form,
Spewing its ink with ravaging passion
Into the womb that is the blank page
The breeding ground
For the conception of ideas.
Letters.
Lexicon.
Language.
Love.
Laughter.
Light.
Magic.
Giving birth to immortal life,
Authentic and unadulterated,
The soul's gift to the universe.

Overdue Thank You Notes

You have exposed me to the beauty of the world.
When I am lost, you show me the way.
You uncover the darkness.
The light around me is your present to me.
You helped me make my house a lovely home.
If I'm ever bored, I know you'll be there
Igniting my imagination.
You give me the luxury of enjoying a book.
Of recognizing a friendly face.
Thank you, eyes.

Whenever I'm stressed, I can count on you.
A comforting voice, a good laugh, or a soothing
song.
You give me all of these and more.
Thank you, ears.

When I have something to say,
You always ensure that I'm heard.
You help me connect with others
And make my mark on the world with my words.
Thank you, voice.

I know you'll always support me.
When I'm down, you'll pick me up.
You hold the weight of all my burdens.
No matter how much I put on you,
you can handle it,
Never once letting me down.
You are my strength to stand tall.
Without you, I'm truly nothing.
Thank you, back.

You keep me satisfied like nothing else can.
Giving me the fuel to get through each day.
If something's not right, you'll let me know.
You take in all that will make me better
And gracefully eliminate what no longer serves.
Thank you, gut.

You wrap me in a warm embrace.
A letter, a poem, a painting,

I owe you for the gifts I grant others
Because my creativity is the gift you grant me.
Thank you, hands.

You take me out
And ask me to dance.
If ever there's danger, you'll make sure I get away.
I can go anywhere with you,
And you'll always get me home safe.
Thank you, feet.

I have had many addresses throughout my life,
Spread across states and continents.
But you have and always will be my constant.
My permanent residence.
My soul's home in this lifetime.
Thank you, body.

A Thousand Lifetimes

Lying together, we intertwine.
Between our bodies, there are no lines.
We begin to unwrap each other's minds,
Learning their inner workings, seemingly
clandestine,
Yet intuitive to friends of a thousand lifetimes.
My heart becomes yours, and yours becomes mine.
You intoxicate me more than wine
With your words and your smile, so sweet and
sublime,
Reminding me that everything is just fine.
When we met, the stars aligned,
I instantly *saw* you, friend of a thousand lifetimes,
Rekindling a connection most divine,
One that that is rare, one-of-a-kind,
Transcending all space and time.
Night after night, under the moon's shine,
Again and again, our souls intertwine,
Afresh I become all yours, and you all mine.
I will always see you, friend of a thousand lifetimes.

To My Weak Nails

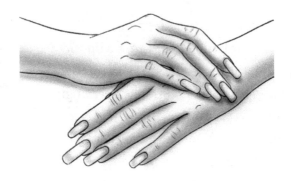

To My Weak Nails~
You take up such a small percentage of my body,
But you have the power to bother me so much.
I can't concentrate on anything else
Because I'm busy fiddling with you
And trying to get rid of you.
You're so tiny,
Yet you are somehow able
To make the entire rest of my body
Uncomfortable.
You are a clear indicator
That I'm stressed
Or have some sort of deficiency.

When I cut you,
I feel immense relief
But also envy
For those who know how to preserve your strength,
Your perfectly edged yet rounded shape,
The elegance and femininity you exude.
Nonetheless, I am glad you are not worse off
And are still able to do your job.
One day, I will give you back your vitality.
Love, ~Me

Not Alone

Anytime you
Open a book,
Watch a show,
Look at a painting,
Listen to a song,
Feel the feelings
Of interacting with creations
And finding yourself within,
The universe is giving you
A reminder
That you are not alone.

Snapshot

How nice it would be
To enjoy a picturesque moment
And take pleasure in it
For its own sake
Without feeling the urge
To snap a photo
For social media
To express
Or impress
Or inspire
And instead
Truly live the experience
And preserve the snapshot
In my mind.
My body.
My soul.

Brave

"You're so brave," they say,
"To travel the world
By yourself
As a young woman."
They mean well,
And I appreciate the sentiment.

But do they not realize
That I am more at risk
Being planted in a place
Where politicians prioritize
Their pockets and profits
Over protection of the people?
That one can't leave home
Feeling secure
That they won't get shot
Where they're supposed to be safe
Or that they won't get assaulted
Walking down the street
For no other reason
Than that the homeless and mentally ill
Lack the support that they need?

Do they not grasp
How unhealthy it is
To live in an environment
Where it is encouraged
To fill your body
With toxic chemicals
And artificial substances,
Thinking that it's food
Because it's all that's available or affordable?

They fail to understand
That depending on a vehicle
As your only method of mobility
Because there are no sidewalks
Or public transportation
Where you live
Or everything is just too far apart
Prevents you from moving as nature intended
And pollutes the air.

How can it be safe
To get sick in a place
Where you have to wait months
To be seen by a doctor
And you can't afford to pay
Your medical bills?

Most importantly,
Everyone should know
That the greatest danger of all
Is to never leave home.
To deprive yourself the chance
Of getting intimate
With the unknown.
With all the hidden corners, alleys, and labyrinths
of the world.
The untasted spices.
The friendships you don't even know you're missing.

Life is the biggest risk factor for death,
But to not live
Is far worse.

Crayon Box

You think that those rare, bright, flamboyant
Colors
Are artificial.
Human invented.
Only to be found in a
Crayon box.
But where do you think that crayon box selection
came from?
Nature.
Those rare colors exist
In real life
Outside of the crayon box.
You just have to get out of your human-made cave
And know where to look.

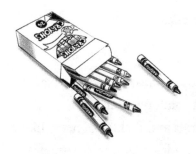

Drive from New York City
To Upstate or New England
In the autumn
And watch the foliage.
Marigold. Cider. Ginger. Honey. Amber. Sandstone.
Golden Gate.
Orange-red. Red-orange.
Orange-yellow. Yellow-orange.

Fly over the Rocky Mountains
From Utah to Colorado.
The sun and rain paint a rainbow in the sky
Against a canvas of cloudy blue-grey. Grey-blue.

Go for a hike deep in the woods,
Farther than you've gone before,
To unexplored terrains.
Fuzzy, radiant green moss
Makes its home
On the branches of the trees.

Make your way up
To the Northern-most tips of the planet
In the dead cold of winter.
Blazing spirals and flickers of neon-like
Dark cyan. Cadet. Medium sea green.

Green-blue. Blue-green.
Illuminate the sky.

Graceful, flowing, dancing swirls
Of eggplant.
Sepia. Saddle. Straw. Spice. Scarlet.
Golden. Hazelnut. Blush. Lipstick.
Bits of cornflower mixed in
Make up the rocks
Of Coloured Canyon
On the Sinai Peninsula.

Dip your toes
Into the translucent, glistening
Crystalline aquamarine waters.
Sparkles in the ocean
In Miami Beach or San Juan
Offering serenity amid the city sonorousness.

Take a stroll
In Central Park.
Every New Yorker's playground and sanctuary.
Popping pink petunia petals pervade.
Absorb the chroma
Of lilacs. Kwanzan cherry blossoms. Crocuses.
Daffodils. Tulips. Forsythia. Foam flowers.

Fritillaria. Crabapple. Grape hyacinths. Azaleas.
Plenty of plants
To uplift any mood.

Plant seeds in a garden.
Nurture your soil.
Nourish your body
With the luscious fruits of your labor.
Fiery tomatoes.
Zesty lemons and limes.
Plump purple berries.
Sustenance and fuel
Served to you by the earth.

Walk outside your home at dusk
And see the hues of salmon, lavender, and orange
Brushing against the sky.
How could you not feel as though you're in a
Watercolor?

Don't let yourself miss
All the splashy shades, tints, and tones.
Let the whole world
Be your crayon box.

Is It Wrong?

Is it wrong
To take pleasure
In being a product
Of systems of power and privilege—
The very same systems
That I'm working to eradicate?

Is it wrong
To crusade against animal cruelty
And climate change
When I'm okay enabling
The burning of fossil fuels
And the emission of carbon dioxide
To fulfill my wanderlust?

Is it wrong
To spend my days
On the ground
Advocating for the needs
Of the most underserved
Only to come home
To wine and dine
In my apartment in the sky?

Is it wrong
To boast about my compassion and empathy
Towards complete strangers
And then often fail
To extend that same courtesy
Toward those closest to me,
Or perhaps even worse,
Towards myself?

Is it wrong?

Why I Write

Connection.
Peace.
Self-Confidence.
Detachment from ego.
Truth.
Impact.
Clarity.
This is why I write.

I'm Not a Tourist

Don't take me to Times Square
Or the Empire State Building.
Take me to play with the squirrels
In Washington Square Park.
To the hidden stone-covered alley of Washington
Mews.
To one of the authentic ethnic restaurants
On the bustling MacDougal Street.
Instead of the fake Little Italy
In Downtown Manhattan,
Let's go to the real one
In the Bronx.
Let's taste the spices
Of Indian street food
And feel the fabrics of the Far East
In Jackson Heights or Richmond Hill, Queens.
And while we're there,
Let's sit in a Gurdwara,
Walking the steps of my ancestors
In the birthplace of the East Coast's Sikh
community.
I want to spend hours

Amid the stacks and shelves at Strand.
Sipping fair-trade coffee at 787.
Vibing with fellow creators at Nook.
Parlaying with locals and foreigners alike.
Listening to the phonemes
Of the mélange of tongues
That all call this place home.
We can take a long hike
In the trails of Forest Hills
Or Inwood Hill Park,
Because as wonderful as Central Park is,
It's far from being
The city's only green space.
We can skip the Statue of Liberty,
Where most visitors just want to take pictures,
Unless it's to dig deep
Into its history
And the stories behind
The hands that built it.
The Met and MoMa are awesome,
But do you know about
El Museo del Barrio?
The Museum of Ice Cream?
The Museum of Sex?
I also love Broadway,

But do you know about
Drunk Shakespeare?
Shakespeare in the Park?
The Comic Strip?
I won't buy souvenirs
From one of hundreds of shops
All selling the same things
But will rather support small businesses
And local artists
Who put their heart and soul
Into their craft.
I didn't come all this way
To sightsee
But to fully appreciate
The depths of a new place
To experience its genotype as well as its phenotype
To live life as a local would
Because I'm not a tourist.
I'm a traveler.

Water

Many people
Feel most connected to the Earth
On the ground,
Walking barefoot in the grass,
Touching the soil.
But never have I felt more connected to the Earth
Than by the water.
After all, the Earth is
71 percent water.

Anytime I feel the tide kiss my legs,
See the ripples radiate outwards,
Ride a boat transporting me between disjointed
lands,
Observe the effortless flow of the waves,
I am in awe of this planet we inhabit.
Whenever I refresh myself
With a glass of water,
I am tasting a piece of home.

Storybook Collection

One of my most prized possessions
Is a storybook collection.
A series of pocket-sized books
Filled from front to back with
A wealth of information
And colorful, intricate illustrations
Telling the tales
Of treasure maps.
Ancestral wisdom.
Coming of age.
Recipes.
Discoveries and adventures.
Unexpected friendships
With people and animals and nature.
Deceptively small in size and word count,
The collection contains the richest of sagas.
This storybook collection
Is my lifetime of
Passports.

To Love a Girl Who Wanders

To love a girl who wanders
Is to never be bored.
To always be ready for an adventure.
To never quite know
What's going to happen next
But being okay with not knowing the answers,
For you are certain
That you're in for a treat.

To love a girl who wanders
Is to constantly be stretched
To new horizons,
Understanding the many ways
That life can be lived
And that no one way
Is truly better than any other.
Just different.

To love a girl who wanders
Is to know that intimacy
Extends beyond the touching of bodies.
That it's possible for the soul

To make love to a place,
Even a place the body has not been,
And feel raw. Aroused. Understood. Safe.

To love a girl who wanders
Is to grasp the inextricable link
Between person and place.
Psyche and space.
Wherever you bring her,
Or more likely, where she brings you,
Will bring out different parts of her personality.

To love a girl who wanders
Is to appreciate
That geography does not dictate
The strength of her relationships.
She is adored wherever she goes
And hangs on to that love when she leaves,
Leaving behind her everlasting sparkle and magic,
Making meaningful connections,
Knowing she has a home to stay
Whenever she comes back.

To love a girl who wanders
Is to always feel at home
Regardless of the walls around you.
She will teach you
That home is in her eyes and in her heart.

To love a girl who wanders
Is for life to forever be enriched.
Seeing the world through different eyes,
And knowing that you're permanently transformed
For the better.

Always There

Even when we aren't talking,
Don't think it's because I do not care.
Remember that I'm always there.
It's easy to get caught up
In day-to-day existence,
Thinking that our humanness
Is our primary form of being
And that our human-to-human interaction
Is what matters most.
But that's not true.
Before we were humans,
We were souls,
And a soul connection
Runs much deeper
Than a human one.
That is why we communicate
In our dreams
And through memories
Of our times shared.
Whenever you see
A butterfly,
A green and pink pattern,

A heart-shaped leaf,
Or anything else that reminds you of me,
That's my soul
Smiling at yours,
Saying hello
And that I'm thinking of you.
So even when we aren't talking,
Don't think it's because I do not care.
Remember that I'm always there.

Artist

What does it mean
To be an artist?
To work on your craft every day?
To create a certain amount per unit of time?
To get paid for your production?
To be featured in public exhibitions?
To be loved or hated by the people?
To make them feel?
To have an impact on social and cultural norms?
Maybe.
Or maybe not.
To be an artist
Means whatever the hell
You want it to mean.

What Do You Do?

"What do you do?"
Is the first question
Almost everyone asks.
What do they want to know exactly?
How I make my money?
How I spend the majority of my days?
Do they really think
They can condense twenty-four hours
Into nine to five
(Assuming that's actually when I work),
Boxing my being into eight hours
And thinking those hours define me?
Maybe they should consider asking instead,
"What makes you happy?"
"What do you like to do?"
"What issues are important to you?"
"What are your goals?"
"How do you leave your sparkle in the world?"

Listen to the Kids

Grownups
Often have the false impression
That they know better.
That the kids should just
Listen.
That's not always true.
Grownups,
Kids are often closer
To the eternal source
Than we are.

We must not forget
That despite their limited experience in this lifetime
And perhaps their limited knowledge,
They are troves of wisdom.
We must remember
That they are not growing up
In the same world
That we did.
No one knows what they're going through
Better than they do.
Sometimes, the kids do know best.
It is our turn
To shut up
And listen.

Ramona Street

Palo Alto, California.
The land of innovation
And intellectual vitality.
Of eighty-hour work weeks.
Competition and burnout.
Conversations dominated by pitches and capital and
tech
Or the invention that's "going to change the world."
Mansions accessible to a select few
And prices ascending faster than airplanes,
Yet still one of the cities I feel most at home
Because of Ramona Street.
The small block between University and Hamilton
Is where I find my element
In the middle of a large city
That I reluctantly admit
Perpetuates the subtlest of toxicity.
A city that unintentionally makes life harder
In the pursuit of making it easier.
Ramona Street.
A block where work-life balance is possible.

Where one can spend an entire day without feeling
exhausted.
Slowly sipping on hot chocolate and savoring
crepes,
Followed by an afternoon of tea served in the finest
china instead of paper cups,
Culminating in an evening of merriment over wine.
Ramona Street.
A block where business is not transactional.
Where people are not their productivity, but their
stories.
Where I can say I make a living as an artist and not
get stares of shock in response.
Where I can cultivate not only a professional
network but genuine friendships.
Community.
Connection.
Ramona Street.
My solace.
My belonging.
My home away from home.
A space that truly can change the world.

Loving Kindness

As you go throughout your day,
Take a minute
To appreciate
The people
Who make possible
The conveniences you enjoy.
The clean streets,
The food on your table,
The water you can drink,
The clothes you wear,
The books you read,

Your ability to move from place to place,
The care you receive when sick or injured,
Your smartphone
Don't come out of thin air
But are the result
Of human efforts.
When you're able to travel
Or go to the supermarket
On Christmas or New Year's,
Remember the employees
Who came to work

Instead of spending time at home
With their own families
Or simply taking a well-deserved break
To make that possible for you.
When the lines are long
And moving slowly,
Don't get angry at the faces in front of you
For not being able to move faster.
Be grateful
That they showed up at all.
Don't forget
That behind any machine or app
Is a person.
A person with their own family.
Their own issues.
Their own stories.
Their own feelings.
Keep this in mind
When you have the urge
To get mad. Frustrated. Upset.
Instead, take a breath
And practice
Loving kindness.

Keep to Myself

Sometimes I find it easier
To just keep to myself.
If others knew the whole truth,
They would worry about me.
The concern of others
Is too much of a burden to carry.

Dance Class

Dance class.
Since 2017,
One of the most important parts of my day.
A pick-me-up.
A gift to my body.
Thirty minutes
To let the beats and lyrics lead.
Whenever I want to bring myself
Back to a particular phase of my life—
The people I loved,
The fights I had,
The passion and the heartbreak and the loss,
Where I was working and what I was doing,
The home where I was living,
The anticipated vacations,
Hotel stays,
Weddings,
Sicknesses,
Funerals,
Births,
Tears shed and laughter shared—
All I have to do

Is hear a song
From my dance playlist at the time,
And everything comes back to me.
The emotions,
The senses,
The moves
So deeply ingrained in my muscles and bones.
My mind can be absolutely anywhere,
As it often is,
But it doesn't matter.
The beats and lyrics play,
And my feelings and my body
Know exactly what to do.

A Day in the Life of an Editor

Lying in bed,
Computer in my lap,
My eyes focused
On the words in front of me
In an effortlessly meditative state
As my fingers tap the keys
Or move the mouse,
And my mind puts my unmatched command
Of the nuances and subtleties of language
To good use.
Crossing out words that don't belong
Or add anything useful,
Correcting misspellings and flawed sentence
structures,
Replacing improper parts of speech,
Shifting misplaced prepositions or entire
paragraphs,
Creating clarity from the unintelligible,
Occasionally feeling frustration
At the mess I've taken on,
But ultimately gaining satisfaction
From converting goodness to greatness,

Enhancing my depth and breadth of knowledge,
Forging friendships with creators
On the other end of the screen,
And giving them the gift of confidence
To proudly share their work with the world.

Breath

Sitting in a yoga class
With multiple other bodies,
Eyes closed,
Breathing together
Synchronously.
Inhale.
Exhale.
Inhale.
Exhale.
I forget that I am in a yoga studio.
Instead, I feel as though I am at the ocean,
Feet dipped in the water,
Listening to the ebbs and flows of the waves
Or at an airport
Hearing the ascent and descent of airplanes,
Reminding me that breath, too,
Is movement.
A journey.

Pure Love

To go to sleep with someone is sexy,
But to wake up with them in the morning is
romantic.
To watch someone strip can make you hot,
But to watch them get dressed fills you with
warmth.
To don elegant attire for a night out is excitement,
But to stay in together in sweats all day is bliss.
To stay up all night talking is exhilarating,
But to revel in the silences,
The simple knowledge of the other's presence,
That's divine.
That's pure love.

Girls' Night Out

Slipping on a tight, lacy, black dress,
The shape of my body resembling a flower vase,
Placing a string of pearls around my neck,
A diamond ring on my finger
Matching the glittery polish
On my meticulously manicured nails,
A shimmering tiara on my head,
And black, high-heeled boots on my feet.
I let my long, dark, freshly washed hair loose
And put on my faux fur coat.
It's time for a glitzy, glamorous
Girls' night out.
Walking outside, taking in the crisp, winter air,
My radiance matches the lit-up trees and buildings.
I enter the lobby of a fancy hotel
Whose ceilings are decked with crystal chandeliers
And walls are lined with velvet sofas,
And ride the lift up to the top floor
To meet my gal pals
At my favorite rooftop lounge,
A classy space

With bookshelves, art, and a fireplace.
I order a glass of pink champagne,
Its bubbling effervescence like my own,
And sway my hips
To the jazz beats in the background.
Together we toast
To our night of glitz and glam,
To laughter shared,
And to memories to be made
And bask in the glory of the evening.

A Love Letter to the Upper East Side

My Beloved Upper East Side~
I couldn't ask for a better place
To call home.
Within you,
I also see myself.

I love you for your eclecticism.
Your beautiful mosaic of modern high-rises,
Pre-war walkups,
And large townhouses
And the various income levels
To which you cater.

I love that you are an introverted extrovert,
Or perhaps an extroverted introvert,
With your melding together of urban activity on
Second Avenue
And pastoral serenity in Central Park or by the East
River.
You attract a vibrant variety of people,
But unlike some of your neighbors,
You are also selective,
Making sure you nurture the right crowd—

Those for whom you will be good,
But also those who will be good to you.

I love you for your creativity
With your mile of museums and galleries
Dedicated to promoting the arts
And your intricate architecture
With wrought-iron swirls decorating the buildings
Or your colorful display of tulips on Park Avenue in
the summer,
Making me momentarily forget
Which city I'm actually in.

I love you because while you have an air of
arrogance
With Billionaires' Row
And your elite prep schools
More expensive than the Ivy League,
Intended to educate future presidents and
entrepreneurs and influencers,
Yet someone failing to fully encourage
Diversity of thought
And eliminate entitlement,
You also have an air of humility.
You know you are classy,

But you don't feel the need
To constantly show off.
Instead, your class is subtle and understated.
That's why you are filled with hidden gems
Not known to all.

I love your kindness to all species
With all your plant varieties in the parks and on Park
And all your spaces for dogs to run and play.
You foster unity
Among all living beings.

Most importantly, I love that you break
So many negative stereotypes
About New York City.
Unlike some of your neighbors,
You are truly a neighborhood.
A community.
A place for all ages and stages and races
With familiar faces
That are remembered and met with warmth and
excitement.

Thank you, Upper East Side.

Love, ~Me

Sunset

After naptime,
Sunset is my favorite part of the day,
Not only because the sky becomes pink—
My favorite color—
But also because we are reminded

That science and art
Are not two distinct disciplines
But are one and the same.
The light is nature's paintbrush,
The electromagnetic spectrum its palette,
The sky its canvas,
And the sunset its masterpiece.

11:11

Magical moments
Twice a day
To pause,
To reflect,
To make a wish.
If you're lucky to catch
These fleeting
Magical moments,
Know that the universe
Is conspiring in your favor.

Butterfly Pose

Sitting on my yoga mat,
I bring the soles of my feet together
To touch each other
And let my knees fall side to side,
Landing as close to the ground as possible.
My attention finds itself
In the small diamond shape
Between my arches.
My thumbs firmly rub
My inner arches,
Which carry much tension
From supporting and transporting
My entire body
All day.
The small diamond shape
Mirrors a larger diamond shape
Formed by my heels, my knees, and my pelvis.
I feel the deep stretch
In my hips and inner thighs
And the release of blocked emotions.

As I shift my spine
From vertical to horizontal,
Becoming one with the ground beneath me,
I am finally able to relax
And fully appreciate
The unbreakable link
Among body, mind, and spirit.

References

1. Johnson, Sharon P. "Butterfly Lore." Baylor University | Lake Waco Wetlands. Accessed January 3, 2023. https://www.baylor.edu/lakewaco_wetlands/index.php?id=34628.

2. Johnson, Sharon P. "Butterfly Lore." Baylor University | Lake Waco Wetlands. Accessed January 3, 2023. https://www.baylor.edu/lakewaco_wetlands/index.php?id=34628.

3. Bremmer, J. M. "Psychē." Oxford Classical Dictionary. March 7, 2016. https://doi.org/10.1093/acrefore/9780199381135.013.5407.

4. "Psyche." Dictionary.Com. Accessed January 3, 2023. https://www.dictionary.com/browse/psyche.

5. Johnson, Sharon P. "Butterfly Lore." Baylor University | Lake Waco Wetlands. Accessed January 3, 2023. https://www.baylor.edu/lakewaco_wetlands/index.php?id=34628.

6. "The History + Meaning of the Butterfly." Alex + Ani. March 18, 2022. https://www.alexandani.com/blogs/the-wire/symbol-meaning-butterfly.

7. Singh, Pavita. "Beautiful: Ode to a Pen." Elephant Journal. September 23, 2015. https://www.elephantjournal.com/2015/09/beautiful-ode-to-a-pen-poem/.

8. Singh, Pavita. "Shut Up, New York." Medium. Accessed January 15, 2023. https://pavitasingh.medium.com/.

9. Singh, Pavita. "More Than the Squares." Medium. Accessed January 15, 2023. https://pavitasingh.medium.com/.

10. Singh, Pavita. "Empowered Woman." Medium. Accessed January 15, 2023. https://pavitasingh.medium.com/.

11. Singh, Pavita. "My Best Friend and My Worst Enemy." Medium. Accessed January 15, 2023. https://pavitasingh.medium.com/.

12. Singh, Pavita. "City Lights." Medium. Accessed January 15, 2023. https://pavitasingh.medium.com/.

13. Singh, Pavita. "Power of the Page." Medium. Accessed January 15, 2023. https://pavitasingh.medium.com/.

14. Singh, Pavita. "My Love Is Mine." Medium. Accessed January 15, 2023. https://pavitasingh.medium.com/.

About the Author

Pavita Singh is a poet and the award-winning best-selling author of *To All the Magic in Me*. Her 20 years of experience as a mental health advocate and world traveler are illustrated through her profoundly relatable collection of poems about the human experience of words, wellness, women's empowerment, and wanderlust.

Pavita is the Executive Director of Girls Health Ed and is currently pursuing her Doctor of Education in Health and Behavior Studies at Teachers College, Columbia University. She is also an instructor at Johns Hopkins University, where she teaches a proprietary class entitled "Self-Care & Storytelling for Public Health Professionals." She holds a Master of Public Health from Yale University and a Bachelor of Arts from New York University. Based in New

York City, Pavita has traveled in 38 countries and 36 US states and territories. Her mission is to spread light, love, learning, and laughter.

To learn more, visit her website at
pavitasingh.com